# FESTIVALS OF THE WORLD

# INDIA

**mc** **Marshall Cavendish**
Benchmark

New York

This edition first published in 2011 in
the United States of America by
Marshall Cavendish Benchmark.

Marshall Cavendish Benchmark
99 White Plains Road
Tarrytown, NY 10591
Website: www.marshallcavendish.us

© Marshall Cavendish International (Asia)
Pte Ltd 2011
Originated and designed by Marshall Cavendish
International (Asia) Pte Ltd
A member of Times Publishing Limited
Times Centre, 1 New Industrial Road
Singapore 536196

Written by: Falaq Kagda
Edited by: Crystal Chan
Designed by: Lock Hong Liang
Picture research: Thomas Khoo

Library of Congress Cataloging-in-Publication Data
Kagda, Falaq.
India / by Falaq Kagda.
p. cm. -- (Festivals of the world)
Summary: "This book explores the exciting culture
and many festivals that are celebrated in India"--
Provided by publisher.
Includes index.
ISBN 978-1-60870-101-8
1. Festivals--India--Juvenile literature.
2. India--Social life and customs--
Juvenile literature. I. Title.
GT4876.A2K24 2011
394.26954--dc22
2009048273
ISBN 978-1-60870-101-8

Printed in Malaysia

1 3 6 5 4 2

# Contents

# It's Festival Time . . .

India is a vast country that is rich in culture. Numerous festivals are celebrated throughout the year. There are festivals for farmers, merchants, and for every religion. With each festival, there's a **mela** [MAY-la], or fair, that goes with it. Come along, take a ride on the Ferris wheel, go on an elephant or camel ride, and buy some dazzling gold jewelry. It's festival time in India!

# Where's India?

India takes up most of southern Asia. It is a huge country that is more crowded than almost anywhere else in the world. One person in every six people on Earth lives in India. The country has the highest mountain range in the world on its northern border and hot tropical jungles in the south. At the heart of India are the Indus and Ganges rivers, which bring water to the dry plains and enables people to live. For this reason and others, the Ganges River is considered to be sacred by many people in India. The capital of India is New Delhi. India also has other very large and crowded cities, such as Kolkata and Mumbai.

## Who Are the Indians?

There are many different peoples and cultures in India. According to some experts, in the sixteenth century, **Aryans** moved from Persia into India, where **Dravidians** were already living. Over the centuries, the two groups blended together, creating the Indian people of today. Indians speak a variety of languages, including **Hindi**, and have widely different customs. Most Indians are Hindus, but there are also many Muslims, Sikhs, Christians, Buddhists, and Jains.

✳ A smiling Indian girl wears a garland of flowers on her way to a festival.

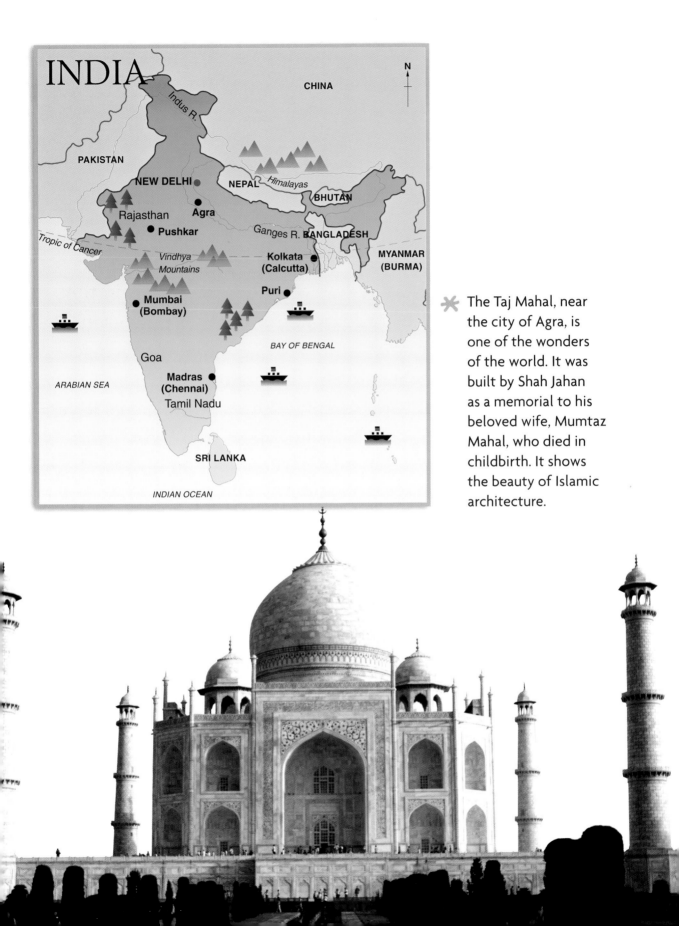

## INDIA

CHINA

Indus R.

PAKISTAN

NEW DELHI

NEPAL

Himalayas

BHUTAN

Rajasthan

Agra

Pushkar

Ganges R. BANGLADESH

Tropic of Cancer

MYANMAR
(BURMA)

Vindhya
Mountains

Kolkata
(Calcutta)

Mumbai
(Bombay)

Puri

BAY OF BENGAL

Goa

ARABIAN SEA

Madras
(Chennai)

Tamil Nadu

SRI LANKA

INDIAN OCEAN

✳ The Taj Mahal, near the city of Agra, is one of the wonders of the world. It was built by Shah Jahan as a memorial to his beloved wife, Mumtaz Mahal, who died in childbirth. It shows the beauty of Islamic architecture.

# What Are the Festivals?

Indians use three different calendars. Hindu festivals follow a special **lunar** calendar. This calendar follows the phases of the moon. The dates of these festivals change from year to year on the Gregorian calendar, which is used in the United States. Muslims follow a different lunar calendar. Their festivals move back eleven days each year!

## SPRING

* **Basant**—For this celebration of spring, people often wear yellow and participate in kite-flying competitions.

* **Mahavir Jayanti**—Celebrates the birthday of Vardhamana Mahavira, who started the Jain religion. Jains come from all over to visit their shrine at Gimar.

* **Holi**—During this spring festival, people throw colored powder and water at each other.

* **Pooram**—A celebration involving a procession of elephants that are decorated with elaborate head ornaments.

* **Baisakhi**—Sikhs celebrate the New Year at this time. They have a big meal at the temple, and then dance the bhangra in the streets in the evening.

## SUMMER

* **Ratha Jatra (The Chariot Festival)**—Images of the god Krishna and his family are dragged through the streets of Puri on huge chariots. It can take four thousand people to pull one of these chariots.

* **Independence Day**—Besides Republic Day, this is another day for India to celebrate its independence from Great Britain in 1926.

* **Raksha Bandhan**—A day to observe the special ties between brothers and sisters.

Come monkey around with me and the other animals during Pooram!

* **Naag Panchami**—This festival pays homage to the Serpent God. On this day, Indians respect and honor snakes, which are believed to offer protection from bad spirits.

# AUTUMN

* **Dussehra**—This festival celebrates the mother goddess, Durga. Statues of Durga are carried to the Ganges River and then thrown in the water.

* **Diwali**—During the Festival of Lights, Indians prepare for a fresh start by dressing in new clothes, cleaning their homes, and lighting lamps to usher in good luck.

* **Pushkar Mela**—People come to bathe in the holy Pushkar Lake and attend a big camel fair.

* **Gandhi Jayanti**—Celebrates Gandhi's birthday on October 2.

# WINTER

Republic Day is a time to celebrate India's road to independence.

* **Guru Nanak Jayanti**—Sikhs celebrate the birthday of Guru Nanak, who started Sikhism.

* **Republic Day**—The more colorful counterpart of Independence Day, in which there are parades and breathtaking air shows.

* **Pongal**—A harvest holiday to celebrate new rice crops. In Southern India, it is also an event to honor the cow, which is considered a sacred animal.

* **Carnival**—Christians in Goa celebrate the carnival with a traditional dance, in which they wear all red and black.

# MUSLIM HOLIDAYS

* **Muharram**—The anniversary of the day the Prophet Muhammad left for Medina, which marks the beginning of the Islamic religion. There are processions in honor of al-Husayn, the Prophet's grandson, who was killed on this day.

* **Id al-Fitr**—This holiday marks the end of the fasting month of Ramadan. People wear new clothes and have big feasts.

* **Id al-Adha**—During the festival, families **sacrifice** an animal, such as a sheep, and share its meat with neighbors and people who are less fortunate.

7

# Republic Day

On January 26 in New Delhi, camels and elephants painted in bright colors parade down the street for Republic Day. In the sky, airplanes put on a thrilling air show. People in wonderful costumes from different regions of India perform traditional dances. Republic Day brings people from all over India together to celebrate their country!

## Come to the Parade

On a low hill in the center of New Delhi is a red sandstone palace where the president of India lives. Below is a grassy mall. This is where the Republic Day parade takes place. Long rows of wooden bleachers are set up for spectators. In the center is an armchair under a gold umbrella where the the president sits to view the parade. Troops of horsemen ride past wearing red coats and gold turbans. Next come the elephants, which are painted with flowers. Soldiers and sailors, boy scouts and girl scouts, and other groups march past in their uniforms.

Then come the floats representing the states of the Republic of India. Each is brightly decorated to show off the best each state has to offer.

✳ This elephant is decorated to march in the parade. National heroes and leaders have the honor of riding on the elephants.

## What Is Republic Day?

Indians actually have two independence days. Republic Day is the anniversary of the day when Indians declared their independence from Great Britain in 1926. India also celebrates Independence Day, the day when the British turned over power to Jawaharlal Nehru, India's first prime minister. On Independence Day, the president makes a speech. However, the real show takes place on Republic Day, when the weather is cool and thousands of people gather to watch the amazing parade.

The camel corps from the desert region of Bikaner is one of the focal points of the parade.

## Independence

Beginning in the nineteenth century, India was a colony of Great Britain, but Indians wanted to be in control of their country. They were concerned that the British were using India and its resources to get rich, while Indians stayed poor. The people of India believed they had to force the British to leave. The British had a very powerful army, however. The Indian people needed help to overcome them, but what could they do?

## A Great Man

Mohandas K. Gandhi was a leader of the Indian struggle for independence. People call him Mahatma Gandhi. *Mahatma* means great soul. He believed that it was wrong to kill other people. He thought the best way to make the British leave was to refuse to obey unfair laws. He called this "passive resistance."

## Make Your Own Salt

When the British put a tax on salt that made it very expensive, Gandhi announced he was going to make salt himself. He started walking to the sea, which was 150 miles (240 kilometers) away. As he walked, people joined him. Finally there were thousands of people marching at his side. After many demonstrations like this one, the British were forced to give India back to its people.

✳ When he was a young man, Gandhi wore pants and shirts. Later in life, he wanted to be closer to the common people of India, so he started to dress like a simple farmer. He also learned how to spin yarn and wore hand-woven clothes.

**THINK ABOUT THIS**

India has been independent for a short time, but it is a very old culture. Indian ideas and Indian stories have affected many countries. In the United States, Martin Luther King, Jr., borrowed Gandhi's idea of passive resistance and used it in the Civil Rights Movement.

✳ Dancers come from all parts of the country to represent their region. Here, a troupe of Sikhs dance the **bhangra** in the parade. Sikh men never cut their hair and cover it with a turban as a mark of their religion. Guru Nanak started the Sikh religion to bring Hindus and Muslims together. He wanted to show people that god was neither Hindu nor Muslim.

✳ Indian dance was at first a way of worshiping the gods. Most dances tell a story about gods or heroes.

## Let's Dance

After Republic Day comes a two-day festival in which people play music and dance. India has its own music and dance forms that go back thousands of years and are admired all over the world. *Bharatnatyam* and *Kathak* are two types of traditional dance. Kathak dancers wear bands with rows of bells on their ankles. As they move, the bells create a wonderful sound.

India is also famous for its beautiful **sitar** music. The sitar is a large stringed instrument that makes an unusual, soothing sound. Ravi Shankar is a sitar player who is famous around the world. The sitar is usually accompanied by the **tabla**, a kind of Indian drum.

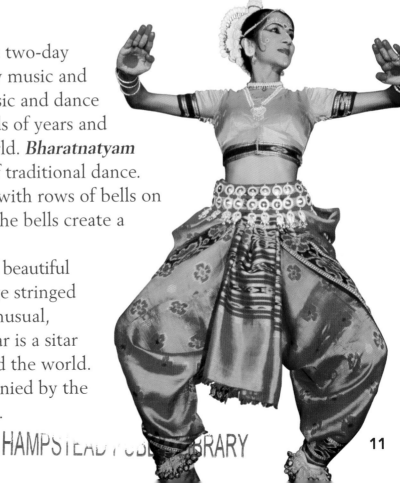

# Diwali

It's late autumn in India, and the moon is only a sliver in the night sky. On the last days of Ashwin —the Hindu month that falls in October or November—rows of small, flickering clay lamps appear in doorways and windowsills. The lamps even light up the outlines of tall government buildings. These are the lights of Diwali [dee-WAL-ly], or the Festival of Lights. Diwali is dedicated to Lakshmi, the Hindu goddess of wealth and beauty. During the five days of Diwali, Lakshmi is believed to visit houses and shops that are tidy and brightly lit. According to the Hindu religion, she brings wealth and good fortune, and most of India is lit up to invite her in.

✳ A Hindu goddess is decorated for Diwali. Hindu gods and goddesses often have several sets of arms, which are thought to be a sign of power.

## A New Beginning

To get ready for Diwali, Indians buy new clothes, bathe in scented water, and clean their homes. They also pay off any debts. Diwali is a time to start fresh, with the hope that Lakshmi will bring better fortune in the coming year. Hindus go to temples to honor the gods. Then they come home and eat special meals. Later they visit family and friends, bringing gifts of sweets. It is traditional to give sweets at Diwali.

## The Demon of Filth

The beginning of Diwali can be traced back to a legend about a demon named Naraka. Naraka was very dirty, so he was called the demon of filth. He kidnapped young girls and took them to live in his filthy house. One of those girls was Lakshmi.

Krishna—one of the most popular Hindu gods—fought with Naraka to free the girls and won. As Naraka was dying, he felt sorry that he had made people unhappy. He asked Krishna to make the anniversary of his death a day when people would be happy. That day became Diwali. People celebrate by taking special baths, dressing up in new clothes, and cleaning.

✳ Fruit, flowers, and sweets are some of the offerings made to the gods.

✳ During Diwali, entire villages are lit up and fireworks are set off to signal the triumph of light over darkness.

13

## The Lights of Goodness

*Diwali* means row of lights. On the long, dark nights of Diwali, the lamps remind people that goodness and wisdom are stronger than the forces of darkness. There are many stories that people tell about Diwali, but all of them are about the triumph of good over evil. Another Diwali story about the victory of good over evil involves an Indian hero called Rama.

Lights invite Lakshmi to bring good fortune. Young Indian children prepare to set Diwali lamps afloat in a river. They believe that if the light burns for as long as they can see it, they will have good luck in the next year.

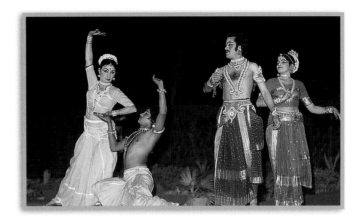

✳ One of the stories that is popular during Diwali is that of the hero Rama. Here people use dance to tell the story of Rama's return to his kingdom. These dance dramas are popular throughout the festivals of Dussehra and Diwali.

## Rama Comes Home

Many Indian festivals celebrate several things at once. Diwali lights also remind Hindus of the story of Rama's return to his kingdom. According to the story, Rama was unfairly sent away from his kingdom. Then the demon Ravenna kidnapped Rama's wife. Rama fought Ravenna to rescue his wife, eventually killing Ravenna. When Rama returned to his kingdom, the people lit lamps to guide him back.

During the holiday of Dussehra [duh-SHEH-rah], which comes just before Diwali, people put up giant statues of Ravenna. At the end of the festival, they put firecrackers inside the statues and set them on fire. On the night of Diwali, Indians light lamps to celebrate Rama's return.

✳ These statues of Ravenna are ready to be set on fire.

# Holi

✻ Some people use special bicycle pumps to squirt red, yellow, and green liquid over everyone.

In India in March, it is not uncommon to see people completely covered in bright colors. This is Holi, and on Holi people walk around yelling, *"Holi hai, Holi hai,"* and throwing colored water or powder at anyone they see. Everyone gets drenched in color, even the mayor! During Holi, everyone is equal and everything is forgiven. The important things are *rang, ras,* and *rag,* or color, dance, and song. So join the fun, throw a little powder, and dance and sing in the streets! This is the festival of colors.

## A Fun Time

On the first night of Holi, young men and boys make a huge bonfire. Then they dance around the fire, sometimes jumping through it, being careful not to get burned. Food that has just been harvested is put on the fire as an offering. The next morning, the fun begins. Besides throwing colored powders and water, there are huge fairs and circuses. People forget their differences and join together in a joyful celebration.

✻ Powders of different colors are offered for sale on the streets. These colors usually wash out of clothes without staining.

# Girls Versus Boys

Near Delhi, the women of one village pretend to have a fight with the men of a nearby village. The women carry long bamboo poles. They try to hit the men with their poles. The men carry leather shields. They dodge through the crowds, trying to escape the women. When the women get tired, the men shout at them to keep the fun going!

## The Holi Story

There are many stories about Holi in different parts of India. The best-known story is about a young prince named Prahlad. Prahlad worshiped the god Vishnu and was very religious. His father, however, wanted to be a god and forced the people, including his son, to worship him. When Prahlad refused to obey, he asked his sister, Holika, to punish Prahlad. Holika had the power to walk through fire without getting burned. One day, she carried Prahlad into a bonfire. People heard terrible screams and thought that Prahlad was burning to death. Finally, Prahlad walked out alone. His faith had protected him, while Holika burned. That's why there are bonfires for Holi today.

## Celebrating Springtime

Holi is also like many other spring festivals around the world. Many people celebrate the return of spring with a noisy festival where people dance and sing. It is a time to celebrate the end of winter and the beginning of spring. In India, the spring wheat harvest takes place around this time of year.

✳ After Holi, people get together in public squares to eat, drink, talk, and watch local folk dances.

**THINK ABOUT THIS**
Does your family do a spring cleaning? In the past, trash was taken out and burned in bonfires during Holi and other spring festivals. This was a way of getting rid of the remains of winter and starting fresh.

✳ Opposite: People also remember the god Krishna at Holi. This is a painting of Krishna as a cowherd. According to legend, as a boy, Krishna was very mischievous, and he stole milk from the milkmaids. To get back at him, they threw colored powder on him. That is why people throw colors at each other during Holi.

# For the Beasts

**A**nimals have an important place in Indian life. The people of India have a great respect for them. There are several festivals in India to honor and thank animals. For Pooram, elephants wear gold head ornaments in a parade. The men riding on the elephants carry brightly colored umbrellas and peacock feathers. Naag Panchami is the Festival of the Snakes. People give milk and flowers to snakes that live in the temples. A special event for camels is the Pushkar Mela.

## Come to the Fair

*Melas*, or village fairs, accompany many religious festivals in India. There are also special melas where people come to trade animals. Dressed in their best clothes, people travel long distances to the fairs. At the fairs, people sell everything from pots and pans to jewelry, fruits and vegetables, and cows, horses, and camels. There are magic shows, street dances, puppets, and circuses. No matter what their religion, everyone enjoys taking part in a mela!

✳ A Rajasthani couple takes a ride around the fair on their camel. Many people from Rajasthan wear traditional clothes that are different from those in other parts of India. Women often wear gold nose rings, like this woman.

## The Camels Visit Pushkar

Once a year, the little town of Pushkar in Rajasthan comes alive with a huge camel fair. People come from the deserts around Pushkar to trade camels and enjoy the fair. There are camel races and beauty contests, just for camels, as well as singing and dancing. Merchants sell everything a camel needs, such as colorful saddles and embroidered cloths covered with little mirrors. In the evening, thousands of campfires light up the desert night, and the enchanting sounds of folk melodies fill the air.

✳ A camel performs a trick for its master.

✳ On the night of the full moon, people take a dip in Pushkar Lake. The lake is sacred to Hindus.

# Pongal

Hindus believe cows are very special animals. They do not kill cows for food. Instead, cows are protected and worshiped. In Tamil Nadu, a province in southern India, Hindus have a festival where they honor cows. It's called *Pongal*, which is also the name of a sweet treat made from rice, milk, and brown sugar. Part of the Pongal festival is to make pongal treats and offer them to the gods. Pongal celebrates the rice harvest, so people use the new rice they have just picked for the treats. After they offer pongal to the gods, everyone enjoys one. Hindus also offer the gods clay statues of horses to thank them for sending rain for the growing rice.

✳ Women take advantage of the holiday to shop in the marketplace. There, they look for flower hair garlands and colorful garments to wear called saris.

✱ For Pongal, many people decorate their front steps. This woman creates a lovely pattern using moistened rice flour.

## Thank the Cows

On the third day of Pongal, it's time to thank the cows. Men and boys gather up all the cows and give them a bath. Then they paint their horns. Blue and gold are favorite colors. The men and boys hang garlands of flowers around their necks and decorate the cows with bright feathers. Often there are parades and music for the cows. They get to eat some of the pongal, too.

## Let's Play Tag

At the end of the day, people have bullfights. However, they don't kill the bull like people do in Spain and some other countries. In India, they put a packet of money between the horns of the bull and garlands of money around its neck. Then men try to snatch the money away. Sometimes it can be a dangerous game and people get hurt.

✱ A cow is dressed in its festival best for Pongal.

# Raksha Bandhan

There is no Mother's Day or Father's Day in India, but there is a day for brothers and sisters. It is called Raksha Bandhan. On this day, sisters tie a bracelet called a *rakhi* [RAH-kee] around their brothers' wrists. The rakhi is supposed to protect the brother from anything bad that might happen in the next year. The sister also puts a dot of red powder on her brother's forehead and gives him treats. In return, the brother promises to care for his sister and gives her a small present.

## Special Friends

Even after they have grown up, women give rakhi to their brothers and make them treats. In return, a man might give his sister a new sari. It is a way of saying that even if they do not always get along, they will not stop caring for each other. Sometimes women "adopt" a brother for Raksha Bandhan. Their adopted brother could be a friend they feel especially close to. They then become "Rakhi brother" and "Rakhi sister."

✳ A group of men show off the rakhi their sisters have given them. Often on Raksha Bandhan, young men spend the day parading around in the streets, showing off their rakhi. It is a great honor to receive a rakhi, since it shows that someone cares greatly for you.

✳ Opposite: This little girl is tying a rakhi on her baby brother. In return, he gives her some fruit and money.

# Things for You to Do

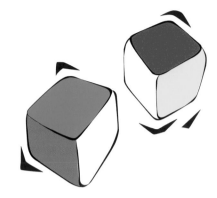

At festival time in India, many people play a game called *Pachisi* [pah-CHEE-see]. It has been played in India for hundreds of years. Indians still enjoy a game of Pachisi today. It takes two, three, or four people to play. Each person needs some kind of playing piece, or token—either yellow, red, blue, or green. Each person will also need a die that is white on two sides and yellow, red, blue, and green on the other four sides. The object of the game is to move all the way around the board and then up the diagonal strip from your home square to the star in the center.

## How to Play Pachisi

Put your playing piece in the corner of the board marked with your color. Have someone throw the die until a color comes up. The person with that color begins. Throw the die. If it comes up the same color as your marker, move one space counterclockwise and throw again. If it comes up white, don't move but throw again. If any other color comes up, your turn is over. The person on your right is next. Play the game until one player reaches the star in the center. The first person to get to the center wins.

## FURTHER INFORMATION

**Books:** *Holidays Around the World: Celebrate Diwali with Sweets, Lights, and Fireworks.* Deborah Heiligman (National Geographic Children's Books, 2008).

*The Little Book of Hindu Deities: From the Goddess of Wealth to the Sacred Cow.* Sanjay Patel (Plume, 2006).

*Stories from India.* Anna Milbourne (Usbourne Books, 2006).

**Websites:** festivals.iloveindia.com—Filled with lots of information covering all of India's major festivals, including rituals, recipes, and much more.

india.gov.in/knowindia/kids.php—The kids corner from India's official website is especially useful for young readers who want to learn more about India's history.

# Make a Diwali Lamp

**M**ake a colorful lamp to light your house at Diwali. Use the kind of clay that hardens by itself. In India, Diwali lamps are filled with oil. Ask an adult helper to help you light up your lamp with a candle.

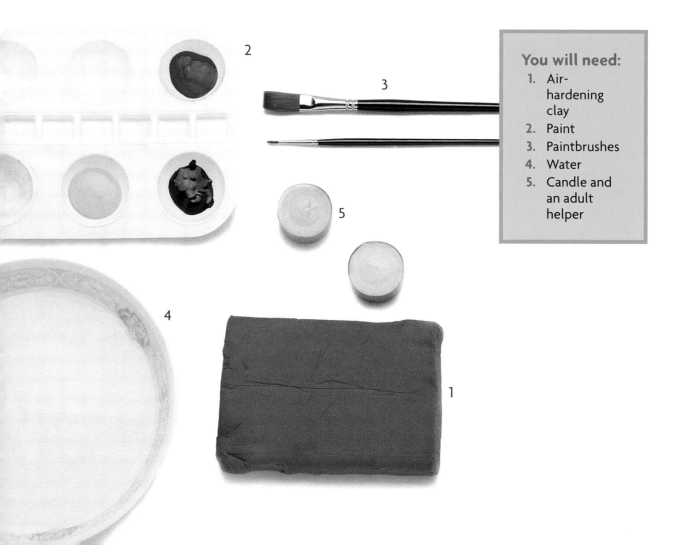

2

3

5

4

1

**You will need:**
1. Air-hardening clay
2. Paint
3. Paintbrushes
4. Water
5. Candle and an adult helper

1 Break off a handful of
clay and roll it into a ball. Knead
it well to make it soft enough to
work with. Wet the clay from time
to time to keep it from drying out.

2 Mold the clay into a lamp shape by
hollowing out the middle of the ball. Keep
working the clay until the sides are the right
thickness. Keep the clay thick around the edge
to form a lip. Make the bottom flat so it won't
roll. When your lamp looks the way you want it
to, set it aside to dry.

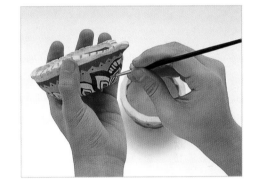

3 When your lamp is completely dry, it is
time to paint it. Use bright colors to make
it look nice and bright. You can put some de-
signs on the inside, too. After the paint has
dried, ask an adult to put a candle inside!

# Make Burfi

Here is a recipe for a simple Indian treat called *burfi*. Try making it for Diwali. There are many kinds of burfi made with different kinds of nuts and flours. After you have tried your own, look for a shop that sells Indian snacks and sample some other kinds!

**You will need:**

1. 1 pound (1⁄2 kg) raw cashews
2. Blender
3. 1 cup (240 ml) sweetened condensed milk
4. Butter
5. Pastry brush
6. 1 teaspoon flour
7. Measuring spoons
8. Small saucepan
9. Frying pan
10. Baking tray
11. Wooden spoon
12. Knife

1 Ask an adult to help you put the cashews in a frying pan and cook them over low heat. Stir them constantly until they are golden brown. Be careful not to burn them!

2 Grind the roasted cashews. You can use a blender or crush them in a bag with a rolling pin.

3 Mix half the ground cashews, the condensed milk, and the flour in a saucepan. With an adult, cook the mixture for a few minutes until it is almost solid.

4 Grease the baking tray with the butter. Press the cashew mixture into the greased pan. Pour the remaining cashews over the top and press them into the mixture. Let it cool, and then cut the burfi into squares.

# Glossary

| | |
|---|---|
| **Aryans** | Fair-skinned people from Persia who settled in India. |
| **bhangra** | A folk dance performed by Sikh men at Baisakhi. |
| **Bharatnatyam** | A traditional dance of India. |
| **Dravidians** | Dark-skinned people who lived in India long ago. |
| **Hindi** | The official language of northern India. |
| **Kathak** | A traditional Indian dance using bells around the ankles. |
| **lunar** | Following the phases of the moon. |
| **mahatma** | A title of respect meaning great soul. |
| **mela** | A fair. |
| **rakhi** | A bracelet sisters give to brothers on Raksha Bandhan. |
| **sacrifice** | To give up something that is extremely precious. |
| **sitar** | An Indian stringed instrument with a long neck. |
| **tabla** | A pair of drums of different sizes used in Indian music. |

# Index